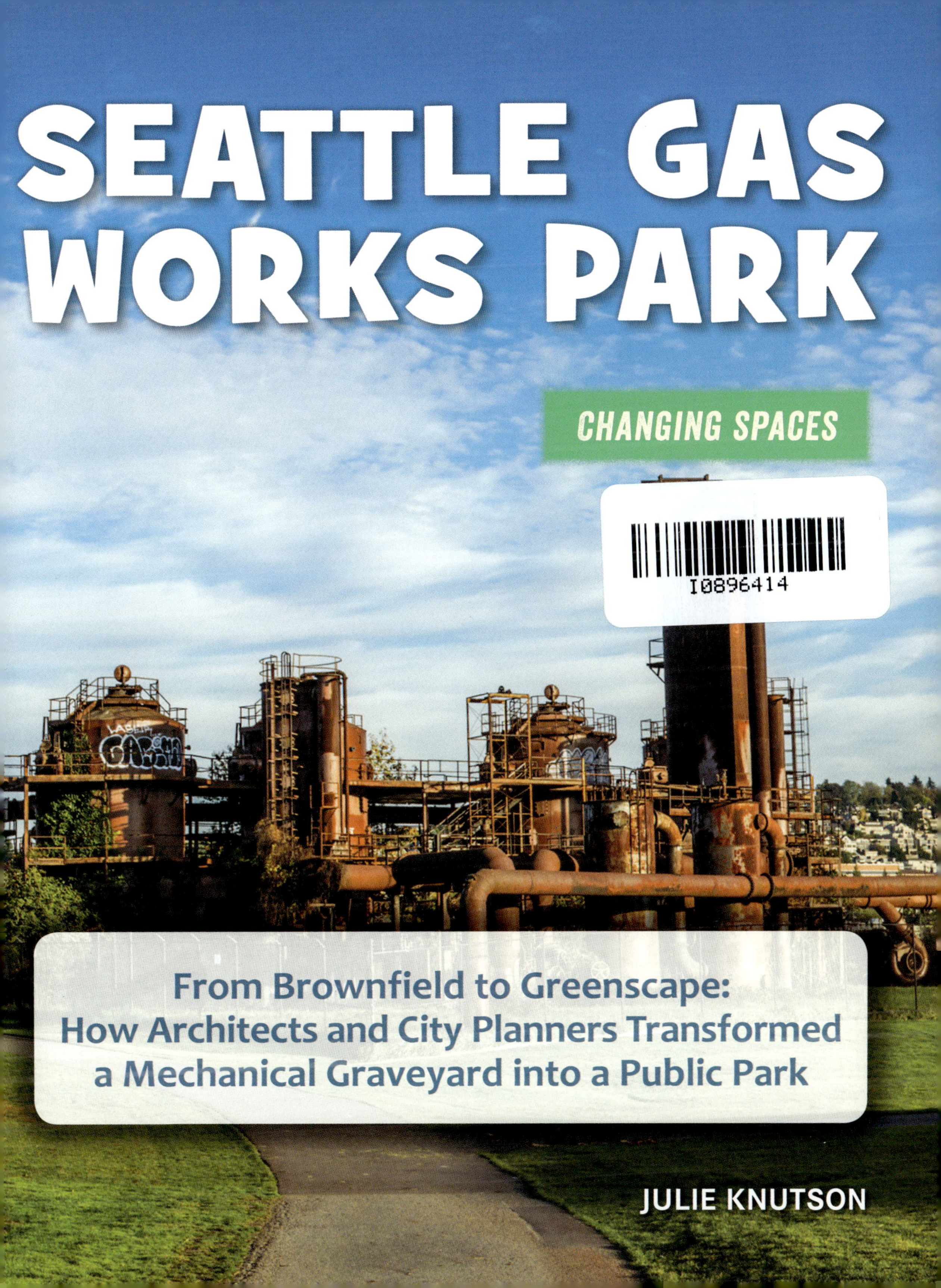

SEATTLE GAS WORKS PARK

CHANGING SPACES

From Brownfield to Greenscape: How Architects and City Planners Transformed a Mechanical Graveyard into a Public Park

JULIE KNUTSON

CHERRY LAKE PRESS

Published in the United States of America by Cherry Lake Publishing Group
Ann Arbor, Michigan
www.cherrylakepublishing.com

Reading Adviser: Marla Conn, MS, Ed., Literacy specialist, Read-Ability, Inc.
Photo Credits: © Checubus/Shutterstock.com, cover, 1, 7; © chirajuti/Shutterstock.com, 5; © Everett Historical/Shutterstock.com, 9, 11; © Max Herman/Shutterstock.com, 15; © alspaige/Shutterstock.com, 16; © Amehime/Shutterstock.com, 17; © Cascade Creatives/Shutterstock.com, 18; © steve estvanik/ Shutterstock.com, 21; © CK Foto/Shutterstock.com, 24; © Jason Finn/Shutterstock.com, 27; © Alice-D/Shutterstock.com, 28

Cherry Lake Press is an imprint of Cherry Lake Publishing Group.

Library of Congress Cataloging-in-Publication Data
Names: Knutson, Julie, author.
Title: Seattle Gas Works Park / by Julie Knutson.
Description: Ann Arbor, Michigan : Cherry Lake Publishing, [2021]. | Series: Changing spaces | Includes index. | Audience: Grades 4-6 | Summary: "Learn more about how Seattle's Gas Works Park went from unused brownfield land to vibrant urban park and art space. Explore the logistics of repurposing the land and meet the people who made it happen. The book showcases a range of 21st century skills—from "Flexibility & Adaptation" to "Creativity & Innovation"—and shows how moving away from a tear-down culture towards one of reuse helps tackle a host of critical challenges facing our planet and population. Thought-provoking questions and hands-on activities encourage the development of critical life skills and social emotional growth. Books in this series include table of contents, glossary of key words, index, author biography, sidebars, and infographics"—Provided by publisher.
Identifiers: LCCN 2020006392 (print) | LCCN 2020006393 (ebook) | ISBN 9781534169012 (hardcover) | ISBN 9781534170698 (paperback) | ISBN 9781534172531 (pdf) | ISBN 9781534174375 (ebook)
Subjects: LCSH: Gas Works Park (Seattle, Wash.)—Juvenile literature. | Land use—Environmental aspects—Washington (State)—Seattle—Juvenile literature.
Classification: LCC F899.S47 G375 2020 (print) | LCC F899.S47 (ebook) | DDC 979.7/772—dc23
LC record available at https://lccn.loc.gov/2020006392
LC ebook record available at https://lccn.loc.gov/2020006393

Cherry Lake Publishing Group would like to acknowledge the work of the Partnership for 21st Century Learning, a Network of Battelle for Kids. Please visit http://www.battelleforkids.org/networks/p21 for more information.

Printed in the United States of America
Corporate Graphics

With thanks to David Graves of Seattle Parks & Recreation

ABOUT THE AUTHOR

Julie Knutson is an author/educator fascinated by the endless ways in which people and communities can transform old spaces for new uses. She lives in Illinois with her husband, son, and extremely energetic border collie.

TABLE OF CONTENTS

Adaptive Reuse—More Than Meets the Eye

Essential Question: *Why create public places that preserve the fingerprints of human history while restoring the natural environment?*

"Since When Has Junk Been Pretty?" This headline screamed from the pages of the January 16, 1972, edition of the Seattle, Washington paper, the *Seattle Times*. The "junk" to which the writer refers? A landscape of abandoned towers and machinery around which the city's newest park would take shape. Many Seattleites harbored similar feelings about the plan to keep these structures. Why not remove all traces of this rusting, toxic gas plant from the proposed recreation zone along Lake Union's north shore? Why preserve these metal objects?

What do you see that is beautiful about these towers?

But landscape architect Richard Haag had a different idea. He felt that the towers should stay. Richard came to this conclusion after camping at the vacant site at his own risk, roaming its grounds by day and tucking into its empty buildings by night. He got to know the space around him and came to see opportunity where others just saw an ugly history to be bulldozed. In his time on-site, the idea of repurposing hulking monuments as playgrounds and picnic spots came to him. He saw beauty in the towers, relics of the city's not-so-distant past. He also thought that the remains of these industrial buildings could remind people of the impact that humans have on the environment. And maybe, it could even inspire visitors to create a more **sustainable** city and world.

Richard knew that the old electricity plant could benefit from **adaptive reuse**. He knew that the oil-slicked, polluted soil beneath it could be decontaminated. He and his supporters just needed to convince City Council and the people of Seattle that it was possible.

The "Jurassic Park of the Industrial World"

In the early 20th century, approximately 1,400 gas manufacturing plants lit streetlamps and homes across the United States. Gas Works Park is the only one of its kind to be preserved, leading Richard Haag to call it "the Jurassic Park of the Industrial World." Because of its unique structures, it was added to the National Register of Historic Places in 2013. Park supporters have also **lobbied** *for status as a UNESCO World Heritage Site.*

After a lengthy battle and a lot of opposing newspaper articles, Richard's side won. In the process, they preserved the last remaining gas manufacturing plant of its kind in the United States. They also provided a **precedent** for preservation and land **remediation** followed by other sites across the globe.

Seattle's Gas Works Park enjoys a reputation as one of the city's—and America's—quirkiest public places.

Today, Seattle's Gas Works Park is a spot where you're just as likely to encounter actors staging a play aboard a pirate ship as kite-flying families and cyclists. It's also a place where you can see and feel how this city has changed over the course of 100-plus years. Let's witness its transformation from the late 19th century to the present.

CHAPTER 1

Lighting a Growing City

Between 1880 and 1890, Seattle grew from an **outpost** of 3,533 people to a sizable town of 42,837. By the 1900 **census**, its population nearly doubled to 80,671. By 1910, 237,194 residents called it home. Economic opportunity—whether through the timber industry, shipbuilding, or mining—drew many to this Pacific Northwest port. During the Klondike Gold Rush, it became a well-known stopping point for fortune seekers about to set off for the Yukon Territory.

Of the 100,00 who left for the Klondike Gold Rush, only about 30,000 made it to the Yukon Territory—and even fewer ever struck gold.

Gold Rush!

Inspired by stories of striking gold, over 100,000 fortune seekers set off for the Yukon Territory in the late 1890s. For many, the first stop was Seattle. The city was publicized as the gateway to the ore-rich North by reporters. Soon, it became a booming port and center of commerce that fed and outfitted aspiring miners at the start of their journey.

Seattleites themselves weren't immune to "gold rush fever." In 1897, while attending a conference in San Francisco, the city's mayor telegraphed his resignation. He then boarded a boat for Alaska . . . without even stopping home first.

In response to these shifts in population, the land that Gas Works Park now occupies also changed. In the 1850s and 1860s, a sawmill operated along Lake Union's shore. From 1890 until 1905, the city used it as a garbage dump to burn waste. With its water access and scenic views, many residents thought it should be reclaimed as a recreation space. In 1903, famed landscape architects John Charles Olmsted and Frederick Law Olmsted Jr. even worked up a plan to convert the grounds into a park. However, industry and economics won out, and in 1905, Seattle Gas Company acquired the land.

The company built a plant to convert coal to gas for lighting, powering the young city's growth spurt. As the first decade of the century turned into the second, new technologies that also required gas—like refrigeration—emerged. By 1930, the **utility** company fulfilled a range of heating, cooling, lighting, and cooking needs across the region, piping gas through more than 1,000 miles (1,609 kilometers) of lines. In the late 1930s, the **natural resources** and technology used to generate electricity changed. Instead of coal, oil was now being converted into gas.

The Aurora Bridge over Lake Union was built in response to the city's booming population. It was finished in 1932.

Seattle on the Map: The 1962 World's Fair

In 1962, at the height of the **Cold War**, Seattle hosted the World's Fair. Nearly 10 million people attended this April-to-October **exposition**. Since the first World's Fair in London in 1851, people from around the world have gathered every few years in a set location to view the latest developments in science, industry, and culture. Entire cities-within-cities have been built to showcase exhibits from participating nations.

The Seattle World's Fair, also known as the Century 21 Expo, centered on the theme of "Man in the Space Age." Fair organizers highlighted aeronautics, NASA's achievements, and other developments in transportation and technology. Iconic landmarks from the fair still loom large over the city. The Space Needle is one, built for the half year of festivities. This futuristic 605-foot (184-meter) tower featured a rotating restaurant and sweeping views. Today, almost 60 years later, it still draws visitors to its observation deck.

The company's operations continued, but by the early 1950s, technology again shifted. Cleaner, easier-to-produce natural gas made the plant out-of-date. In 1956, production ceased.

As the gas plant fell into disrepair, the city around it pulsed on. The airplane manufacturer Boeing made Seattle its home and the center of **aeronautical engineering**. Events like the 1962 World's Fair raised the city's profile as an **innovation** center. Efforts to preserve historic structures and expand the parks system were underway. As part of this push, leaders started to think about giving the former gas plant a new life.

The Olmsteds—Landscape Design's First Family

New York's Central Park, the National Zoo in Washington, D.C.—many of America's most beloved landscapes were designed by Frederick Law Olmsted and his sons, John Charles and Frederick Law Jr. Architect Daniel Burnham once remarked about Frederick Sr.: "An artist, he paints with lakes and wooded slopes; with lawns and banks and forest-covered hills; with mountainsides and ocean views."

CHAPTER 2

A Vision for an Industrial Relic

A half century of electrifying the city took a major environmental toll on the land. The site of the old gas company was a **brownfield**, oozing with toxic pollution. Between 9 and 14 feet (3 and 4 m) of sludge slicked the grounds. The abandoned, metal machinery rusted in pools of muck. It was a ghost town of massive, vacant buildings.

The land stewed in this condition for years. Then, in 1962, the City of Seattle began purchasing it on a 10-year **installment** plan. With the World's Fair in town, politicians and citizens alike reflected on what they wanted their city to be—at that moment

A brownfield is a site contaminated by environmental toxins.

The Olmsted brothers designed the road systems in Acadia and several other National Parks.

Today, Lake Union is one of Seattle's most popular destinations for locals and tourists alike.

and into the future. The notion of a grand, green city park similar to the Olmsted brothers' original plan reemerged. It was hoped that when the city fully acquired the 20.5-acre (8.3-hectare) site in 1973 at a price of $1.3 million, the beauty of the natural landscape would be restored. It would, in City Council's vision, "transform Lake Union from an eyesore to an eye-catcher."

Seeing a project from a different perspective can help initiate new ideas.

Landscape designer and professor Richard Haag participated in conversations about *what* to do with the old gas company. But it wasn't until the early 1970s that he introduced his idea to "hang a park on the skeleton of these old, industrial ruins." Initially, Richard viewed the site as many others did. It was hard to see the potential in the **guano**-covered towers of this sooty, smelly, hazardous place. However, after he started doing on-site planning, his views changed.

When Richard began site planning, he sought out the mystery and spirit of the place. He camped on the site and inhabited the landscape. Doing so opened him up to new ideas and possibilities. He came to recognize the beauty and possibility in the "junk" around him. As he told a reporter in 1975, "I suddenly realized that the city's intention to raze the site was all wrong . . . So I decided to launch a campaign to save the **gasworks**."

Richard and his colleagues envisioned a new kind of park for a changing world. In his view, keeping the towers would make for an unconventional public space that would foster creativity and community interaction.

A Vision for a New Kind of Park

The 1971 Master Plan proposed to the City of Seattle spells out the new types of activities envisioned for the park:

> *MIND PLAY: sketching, painting, music-making, singing, people-watching and promenading; FANTASY PLAY: sun and air bathing, moon viewing . . . exploring the space and structures of the gothic gasworks and other treasure hunting . . . KINETIC SPORTS: pole sitting, sailing . . . structure and pipe climbing and sliding (ironeering) . . . TABLE SPORTS: cards, billiards, skittles, eating and drinking . . . COMPETITIVE SPORTS: bait-casting, bocce ball, croquet . . . SOCIAL PLEASURES: shopping, art . . . ballet, symphony, opera, conventions, conferences, experimental and action theatre, fireworks celebrations, parades, multimedia rock festivals.*

Much of Richard's 1971 plan for the park has been realized. How many of the activities on page 20 do you see here?

Transforming a toxic wasteland into a city park required more than presenting sketches on paper. First, an unconvinced public would need to be sold on the idea of maintaining the gas towers. To address this, Richard invited Seattle's residents to engage in the design and planning process. He opened a studio on-site, offering tours of the grounds and opportunities to explore the industrial ruins. This allowed visitors to experience the site's possibilities in a hands-on way.

Even after convincing the public and City Council to move forward with the plan, additional problems needed to be solved. Fifty-plus years of contaminants nested in the soil. One scientist who visited the site remarked, "They'll never get anything to grow here. It's like the landscape of the moon." But Richard sought advice from experts for strategies to mend the grounds. Through **aeration** and **bioventing**, they filled the soil with oxygen. Organic materials were layered atop the ground to promote the growth of existing microorganisms. This natural process broke down pollutants. Sludge that was too toxic to clean was compacted into the Great Mound, now known to locals as Kite Hill. This and other grass-covered slopes were designed to steer rainwater throughout the park, helping the site heal itself.

How Do You Clean Contaminated Soil?

Scientists employ a number of strategies to clean polluted land, air, and water. Both aeration and **phytoremediation** were used to extract chemicals and waste from Gas Works Park.

What does each process involve?

- Bioventing involves injecting air into the soil. This enhances the ability of naturally present microorganisms to degrade pollutants. This aeration strategy can even break down petroleum products, like gasoline, kerosene, and fuels. While affordable and relatively fast, it isn't effective in all types of soil.
- Phytoremediation draws on plant power to clean up contaminated soil, air, water, or sediment. Certain trees and plants can extract, degrade, and immobilize toxins. This is a slower process than bioventing that requires specific climate conditions. Plants also have a limited capacity to absorb contaminants.

About 5 percent of the original gasworks still stand.

Choices were also made about which structures to keep and which to demolish. Richard and his team reached these decisions based on a number of factors. Were the towers visually interesting? How did they frame the view of the lake and the city beyond? Were they safe to touch and structurally stable? Could they be adaptively reused for other purposes, like a play structure or shelter?

After more than a decade of planning and negotiations, Gas Works Park was officially named on March 8, 1974. When it opened to the public in 1975, it was a place where the city's past and present mingled. It was hoped that this salvaged piece of land would spark creativity, community, and innovation.

CHAPTER 3

A Park with a Unique Identity

Gas Works Park has been an official part of the Seattle landscape for over 45 years. Richard Haag's dream of a park that would provide recreation space for everything from zany, creative enterprises to holiday celebrations has been largely realized. As City Planner David Graves notes, there's "something unique in the character of the park and the former towers that changes people's view of it and encourages one-off, unique pop-up events and actions."

The existence of the old gasworks makes the Seattle park a wholly unique experience.

Old Industrial Sites: Not for Casual Exploration

Old warehouses and abandoned chemical plants are filled with hazards and toxins. It took the City of Seattle years of work with experts to make Gas Works Park safe for visitors. Similar, unremediated sites are definitely NOT playgrounds for casual exploration.

The Landschaftspark in Germany shares many of the same characteristics as Seattle's Gas Works Park.

Today, some remediation work remains to be done. Cleaning up subsurface contamination along the shoreline is a current priority. This would allow visitors to access Lake Union's waters and gain a new view of the park's metal artifacts. Other plans, like the addition of a camera obscura and planetarium, are more remote possibilities. It's up to future generations of design and engineering visionaries to find a way to make these—and other ideas yet to be imagined—a reality.

A Global Inspiration

Gas Works Park inspired similar public spaces elsewhere, including Landschaftspark in Germany. Designed in 1991, this park also encourages reflecting on the industrial past rather than erasing it. The site features light installations, rock-climbing walls, scuba diving pools, and public gardens.

Extend Your Learning

Many supporters of Gas Works Park have called for adding it to UNESCO's list of World Heritage Sites. Research this program and answer the following questions:

- What is UNESCO?
- When and why did the World Heritage Site program begin?
- What World Heritage Sites are in North America?
- How does a site qualify for World Heritage status? Who decides if it should be added?

Write an opinion piece stating your view on whether or not Gas Works Park should be granted UNESCO status. And think about this: are there places in your community that would qualify as World Heritage sites? If so, make your case for their inclusion.

Glossary

adaptive reuse (uh-DAP-tiv ree-YOOS) reusing a structure for a purpose other than that which it was originally designed to serve

aeration (air-AY-shuhn) introduction of air into a material

aeronautical engineering (air-uh-NAW-tik-uhl en-juh-NEER-ing) the job of designing and building aircraft

bioventing (bye-oh-in-VENT-ing) injecting oxygen into soil to stimulate the disintegration of toxins

brownfield (BROUN-feeld) a site contaminated with environmental toxins

census (SEN-suhs) a measure of the number of people living in a certain area in a given year

Cold War (KOHLD WOR) a 45-year period of tense rivalry between the United States and Soviet Union that started in 1947

exposition (ek-spuh-ZIH-shuhn) a large public fair or exhibit of goods and art

gasworks (GAHZ-wurkz) a plant for manufacturing gas

guano (GWAH-noh) bird or bat droppings

innovation (in-uh-VAY-shuhn) a new idea or invention

installment (in-STAWL-muhnt) payment made regularly over a set period of time for something purchased

lobbied (LAH-beed) tried to influence a politician or public official about a specific issue

natural resources (NACH-ur-uhl REE-sors-iz) materials taken from the environment and used for economic gain, such as wood, water, or metals

outpost (OUT-pohst) a town in a remote area

phytoremediation (fye-toh-rih-mee-dee-AY-shuhn) correcting soil contamination through the use of plants and trees

precedent (PRES-ih-duhnt) something done that sets the standard for things that follow

remediation (rih-mee-dee-AYE-shuhn) the act of fixing or remedying a problem

sustainable (suh-STAY-nuh-BUHL) able to be continued in a way that doesn't use up natural resources

utility (yoo-TIL-ih-tee) a basic service supplied to a community, such as water, electricity, or sewage treatment

INDEX